Original title:
Tales of Treetop Travelers

Copyright © 2025 Creative Arts Management OÜ
All rights reserved.

Author: Evelyn Hartman
ISBN HARDBACK: 978-1-80567-263-0
ISBN PAPERBACK: 978-1-80567-562-4

The Leafy Odyssey

In a world where branches boast,
A raccoon rides a wooden ghost.
With a hat made from a leafy crown,
He cheers as he glides all around.

A squirrel swings with showy flair,
Racing past without a care.
He trips on acorns, what a sight,
Then winks at friends, 'I'm still all right!'

Boundless Heights of Nature

High above in the sunshine glow,
A parrot sings—oh what a show!
He dances on the breezy wire,
While ants below march in a choir.

A goat attempts to climb a pine,
With every leap, it feels divine.
He slips and flips but doesn't quit,
"Just testing gravity a bit!"

Perched upon the Whispering Boughs

Chirping birds plot their next prank,
Hiding nuts in the bossy crank.
A bear walks by, clueless in thought,
Steps on a twig—oh the noise it brought!

The monkeys chuckle, swinging fast,
A chase ensues, oh, what a blast!
They throw a mango, dodge and weave,
Nature's game, oh, make-believe!

Skylark and Squirrel

A skylark sings from heights so grand,
While a squirrel plays in the sand.
"Catch me if you can!" they tease,
A merry dance among the trees.

The squirrel spins with glee and grace,
The lark dives low, picks up the pace.
They laugh and race, their joy so clear,
In every branch, they spread their cheer.

Feathered Friends in Upper Edens

In branches high, they caper and play,
With flaps and flutters, they brighten the day.
The squirrel tries to dance, oh what a sight,
As a parrot squawks jokes that just feel right.

A robin with sass gets her friends all in line,
While a pigeon claims it can out-dine the swine.
With chirps like laughter and tweets like cheer,
These feathered pals bring joy far and near.

Navigating the Nesting Heights

With tiny wings, they plot their ascent,
Chasing clouds with giggles, how time is spent.
A bluejay argues over twig and bow,
While a sparrow just laughs, 'Hey, give it a go!'

From nest to nest, they zip with glee,
Sharing tales of mischief, as wild as can be.
Who knew the heights could be such a blast?
When every flight feels like a comic cast.

Flashes of Color in the Woodland Sky

Through leafy branches, colors explode,
A rainbow parade on a bustling road.
The finches are gossiping; oh, do they jest,
While wily raccoons plot their next big quest.

A clownish peacock struts, tail feathers wide,
Each step a wink, like a playful pride.
The sun sets slowly, painting all in gold,
As their antics unfold, each moment retold.

Sagas from the Skyline

Up, up they go, over rooftops and trees,
With squawking and squealing carried on the breeze.
A crow tells a tale of a cat's crazy leap,
While a sleepy owl just wishes for sleep.

In this aviary circus, joy knows no bounds,
With each little flutter, laughter resounds.
On treetop stages, they share their bright dreams,
Turning dull twilight into bright, bursting beams.

The Harmony of Heights and Horizons

In the branches high, a squirrel sings,
Chasing shadows, flapping wings.
A parrot laughs at the monkey's slip,
While a wise old owl plans a trip.

With acorns dropped and giggles shared,
The forest friends, they were well-prepared.
Swinging through leaves, tales come alive,
In the treetop dance, they really thrive.

Tales from the Upper Canopy

Bouncing beavers make a fuss,
While a sloth misses the morning bus.
Raccoons play tag, what a sight,
Under the moon, they dance in the night.

A nimble fox joins the fun parade,
Wearing a hat, in sunshine, he's swayed.
While chipmunks blend their funny acts,
In the comedy club, they gather facts.

The Roosting Rituals of the Aviators

Birds gather for their nightly cheer,
With a trumpet sound, they draw near.
A penguin's lost in the tall pine,
As he complains, we laugh and dine.

With feathers ruffled in funny ways,
They crack jokes in a playful haze.
An eagle swoops for a snack too bold,
And all the others, their stories unfold.

Mysteries of the Forest's Skyline

What's that rustle? Was it a breeze?
Or a bear who's stuck in the trees?
A gopher peeks, an acorn in tow,
But trips on a vine and off he goes.

A hedgehog spins in a leafy twist,
While bees debate who's the best at this.
At sunset's glow, the laughter rings,
As creatures share their funniest things.

Midst the Boughs of Enchantment

In a world where squirrels plot,
They wear tiny hats, like it's all for a lot.
Acorns rain down, a nutty parade,
While chipmunks dance, their antics displayed.

The wise old owl gives a wink,
As birds on branches laugh and sync.
Twirling leaves, like confetti in play,
In this leafy circus where fun holds sway.

The Symphony Above the Ground

The frogs play jazz on the vine,
While crickets tap their toes in time.
A turtle DJ spins records on bark,
As shadows dance, there's a lively spark.

With raccoons in shades, grooving with flair,
They shuffle along without a care.
Singing the chorus of nature's delight,
In this high-up concert, all feels right.

Moonlit Retreats in Leafy Hideaways

Under the glow of a big shiny moon,
A bear in pajamas hums a soft tune.
Bats make headlines as they swoop low,
While rabbits giggle, stealing the show.

Fireflies sparkle, like stars let loose,
While owls debate which path to choose.
The nighttime frolic, so cheeky and bright,
In this secret realm, full of pure delight.

Vibrance of the Upper World

High in the branches, on swings made of vines,
Monkeys sip honey from funny-shaped pines.
Parrots do stand-up, with jokes squeaky clean,
As the forest explodes with laughter unseen.

A hedgehog twirls, pushing leaves all around,
With laughter so loud, it shakes the ground.
In this upper world, where quirks are the norm,
Every creature joins in, a whimsical swarm.

Above the World

In the branches where squirrels plot,
Acorns drop in a nutty lot.
Birds in bow ties sing with glee,
Swinging high, oh let it be!

Lizards dance on the twirling vines,
Spinning tales of adventurous times.
Bugs wearing hats trod on leaves,
While mischief wraps as fun retrieves.

Rain drops land like tiny bombs,
Splatting down on the chirpy psalms.
With every splash, a giggle flies,
As umbrellas bloom in the skies.

Jokes are whispered by the breeze,
Tickling bark-stripped ancient trees.
Nature laughs, and we all jest,
In the treetops, joy's the best.

Below the Stars

Moonlit nights with shadows creep,
Whimsical dreams refuse to sleep.
Owls in glasses read the night,
While fireflies twinkle, oh what a sight!

In the quiet, raccoons laugh,
Playing chess on a fallen calf.
With every move, they scold and cheer,
Inventing games loud for all to hear.

Frogs in coats croak serenades,
As starlit laughter serenely wades.
The crickets drum in funny beats,
While nature dances on quiet street.

Under stars, the stories grow,
Of mischief wrought in moonlit glow.
A campfire's crackle, chirps and hoots,
Our nighttime escapade, oh how it roots!

Flights of Fancy in Leafy Realms

A parrot wears a feathered hat,
Squawking jokes, and how about that?
Fluttering, they make quite the show,
As acorns tumble, the laughter flows.

A snail on stilts goes for a stroll,
While ladybugs spin and take a poll.
In leafy realms of sweet delight,
Each creature's antics steal the night.

Worms in rugby games do play,
Slipping, sliding, what a display!
With muddy smiles, they joyfully flip,
Nature's comedy on a single trip.

Between the trunks, they chase and weave,
In leafy realms, oh, who would believe?
Every leap brings a giggling cheer,
In this funky world, there's no fear!

Chronicles of the Woodland Wanderers

The bear wears shoes that squeak and squeal,
Stumbling as he tries to kneel.
With every step, the forest shakes,
And squirrels giggle, heartily breaks.

Deer with glasses read the maps,
Making routes for friendly chaps.
While porcupines give out sharp advice,
"Don't wander far into the mice!"

The raccoon chef cooks with flair,
Whipping up a dish, a crazy scare.
With pickled nuts and berry stew,
He serves it up for all in view.

Round the bonfire, tales are spun,
Of mishaps, pranks, and gloomy fun.
In woodland whispers, laughter swells,
As every wanderer shares their spells.

Canopy Conspiracies

Up in the canopy, whispers abound,
Critters plot, their secrets have found.
"Who ate the berries?" one squirrel cries,
While the raccoon grins with twinkling eyes.

The birds hold meetings, they squawk and scheme,
Over crumbs they've stolen, inducing a theme.
With tiny goggles, the chipmunks spy,
"Operation Snack-time!" they all reply.

A hedgehog rolls out a plan so neat,
Creating a party with worms as the treat.
Under the moon, the excitement stirs,
As shadows flit from furs so furred.

Giggles explode in the leafy glen,
As mischief mingles with every friend.
In the canopy, laughter takes flight,
As secrets unfold in the silver night!

The Hidden Highways of Nature

Up high where the squirrels play,
Nuts roll down like they're on a sleigh,
With acorn maps that lead the way,
Each twist and turn brings a new display.

Trees wear hats of leaves so bright,
While owls gossip through the night,
A raccoon scales with all his might,
As if he's training for a flight.

Ladders made of vines and bark,
A secret route that leaves its mark,
With every leap a little spark,
A band of critters, bold and stark.

So come, my friend, and join the fun,
With chipmunks dancing, everyone,
Where laughter echoes, no need to run,
In hidden highways, joy's begun.

Whimsical Wanderings Underleaf

In the shade where shadows blend,
Little bugs become a friend,
They spin tales that never end,
Beneath the leaf, they love to lend.

With ladybugs in polka dots,
And fireflies drawing tiny plots,
They play hide and seek in spots,
While grasshoppers hop in funny knots.

A caterpillar's fancy dress,
By lunch, it's surely quite a mess,
He twirls and twirls, oh what a stress,
In a world that's full of zestness.

As clouds drift by and giggle loud,
The canopy forms a cozy shroud,
With every critter feeling proud,
In whimsical walks, we dance a crowd.

The Mystique of Prowling Peekers

At dusk, when shadows stretch and yawn,
Peeking critters greet the dawn,
With bushy tails and sneaky brawn,
They tiptoe soft on velvet lawn.

The raccoons wear their mischief hats,
While possums hide from barking brats,
Each rustle brings on secret spats,
With laughter shared among the chats.

Bats swoop low, with playful dives,
They swoosh through air like giggling jives,
In this world, the whimsy thrives,
Prowling peekers, the joy derives.

Oh, join the crew of sneaky sights,
In moonlit dances, silly flights,
With squeaks and chirps in joyful heights,
The mystique of night surely excites.

Frolics Under the Starlit Canopy

Beneath the stars, the fun begins,
With creatures wearing silly grins,
Frogs croak out their jazzy sins,
While cricket bands play soft violins.

An owl hoots a raucous tune,
While raccoons prance like they're at noon,
Jumping high to reach the moon,
In frolicking steps, we all attune.

The night unfolds with all its goofs,
In shadowed corners, laughter woofs,
With fireflies dancing from their roofs,
Creating joy in dazzling hoofs.

So linger here in nature's play,
Where whimsy leads us all astray,
Under the starlit canopy's sway,
The frolics spark a bright bouquet.

Sorcery of the Spruce

In the branches high, a squirrel took flight,
Sprinkling giggles under moonlight bright.
With acorns as wands, they danced with glee,
Casting spells with a bark and a chuckle free.

Their giggles echoed through the leafy maze,
As they turned the night into a playful craze.
With each little leap, their laughter would soar,
Enchantments of joy, who could ask for more?

Majestic Heights We Call Home

Cackling creatures on lofty peaks,
Swinging from branches, perfecting their tweaks.
A parrot wears glasses, a wise ol' fool,
While the raccoons play teacher, showing the rule.

In dandelion hats, they throw a grand bash,
With fruit punch and snacks, they all made a splash.
Bouncing and laughing, the heights do embrace,
In the canopy's laughter, we find our own place.

The Roaming Raccoon's Chronicles

A raccoon named Ricky, with mischievous paws,
Wrote tales of mischief that earned him applause.
He'd sneak into kitchens with bold little grins,
And leave with a cookie, while the fun just begins.

He plotted grand heists with friends in the trees,
Donned capes made of leaves as they floated in breezes.
Through twinkles and sparkles, their adventures unfold,
With laughter and joy, and stories retold.

A Voyage Among the Verdant Giants

Set sail on a ship made of leaves and dew,
With a crew of blue jays and one kangaroo.
Exploring the trunks that tickle the sky,
They laughed at the clouds as they floated by.

Through the branches, they sailed, a joyful parade,
With acorns for anchors and sunshine displayed.
They toasted the breeze with nutty delight,
As they roamed through the trees, all shimmering bright.

Adventures in the Canopy

A squirrel in a cape, oh what a sight,
He tries to take off, but he's lost in flight.
The birds laugh aloud, they flap and tweet,
While he lands with a thud, right on his seat.

With acorns as hats, the mice do a dance,
They twirl on a branch, oh, what a chance!
A disco in the trees, glowing leaves all around,
As the raccoons join in, they're joyously bound.

The Forest's High Embrace

A monkey named Lou had a banana that slipped,
He soared through the air, oh, what a trip!
He tangled in vines, in a twist and a twirl,
While the owls hoot out, 'What a wild whirl!'

The smelly old skunk starts to mimic a mime,
Waving his paws in a rhythm, so sublime.
But one little misstep, and oh, what a stench!
The comedians scatter, all of them quench!

Secrets of the Sylvan Heights

A parrot tells jokes that fall flat as a leaf,
Yet, every old tree knows, laughter's the chief.
The hedgehog just chuckles, his prickles all sway,
As clumsy old owls mistype on their hay.

A secret cabal of ants throw a spree,
Throwing crumbs in the air, just glee in the spree.
They hustle and bustle, with crumbs on their hats,
Painting the trees with the best of their chats.

Echoes from the Branches

The raccoon with shades thinks he's super cool,
He slides down a branch, oh, what a fool!
He flips on his back, and the leaves all cheer,
While the chipmunk takes bets, 'Is he hurt? Never fear!'

The wise old tree frog hops high and low,
Cracking up the crowd with his green, funny show.
With a leap and a splash, he slips on a log,
And the deer laugh so hard, they all start to jog.

Whispers from the Canopy

Squirrels plot in hushed delight,
While acorns tumble, quite a sight.
They wear tiny hats, oh what a jest,
Planning a feast, they never rest.

A parrot squawks with glee and flair,
Raccoons join in with quite a scare.
Swinging low with a cheeky shout,
They dream of snacks and silly clouts.

A chipmunk dance beneath the sun,
Who knew that critters could be this fun?
With berries piled upon their heads,
They giggle softly and prank their beds.

From branch to branch they hop and glide,
In this leafy realm, they must abide.
With whispered jokes and silly games,
Their laughter sounds like joyful flames.

Soaring Dreams Among the Leaves

A bumblebee buzzed with a plan,
To outfly an owl, oh what a fan!
With tiny goggles and a brave little heart,
He zooms through the treetops, the quirky start.

Nuts and twigs built into a plane,
A squirrel pilot dodges the rain.
With acorn bombs ready to drop,
Their aerial stunts would never stop.

A raccoon co-pilot, strict yet sweet,
Charts the course, can't handle defeat.
Through branches they twist and they turn,
In the game of life, there's always a churn.

They glide on whispers, with wings made of dreams,
Chasing sunlight, collecting wild themes.
A celebration of antics, they cheer and laugh,
In the skyward boughs, they found their path.

Adventures in the Skyward Boughs

An owl in glasses reads all night,
While a hedgehog dons a cape, what a sight!
Climbing high for berries, a daring race,
The tree's a kingdom, they own this place.

A raccoon steals a snack, then starts to dance,
Spinning 'round like he's found romance.
With squirrels watching in pure delight,
They join the fun, no need for fright.

Monkeys swing with raucous glee,
Dropping bananas, oh woe is me!
They paint the leaves with colors bright,
In this playful world, everything feels right.

In skyward boughs, their laughter glows,
Where friendship thrives and mischief flows.
With antics wild, they claim their space,
Nature's playground, their happy place.

The Secret Lives of Arboreal Nomads

With tiny tents hung from a tree,
A raccoon crew throws a wild jubilee.
They roast marshmallows on sticky twigs,
Planning their pranks; oh, what sneaky gigs!

A squirrel's suitcase filled to the brim,
With nuts and tales, oh what a whim!
Traveling far on a leafy route,
In search of mischief, that's the pursuit.

A porcupine dons a feathered hat,
Declaring loudly, "I'm the best at that!"
While owls judge, with their wise old eyes,
In this world of giggles, they've got the prize.

They sing by starlight, a comical choir,
Under the moon, their spirits never tire.
In the trees where their secrets hide,
Adventures bloom, with joy as their guide.

Revelry in the Treetop Realm

In the branches, squirrels dance,
With acorn hats, they prance.
The parrot sings a silly tune,
Underneath the watchful moon.

Monkeys juggling many nuts,
Laughing at their clumsy cuts.
A raccoon slides down a vine,
Declaring it's his party time!

Frogs leap high with joyful glee,
Sipping nectar from a bee.
The wind whispers, always kind,
Tickling leaves that swayed behind.

At dusk they feast on fruits so bright,
Fireflies spark the fun-filled night.
Their laughter echoes far and wide,
In the realm where joy can't hide.

Tales Carried on the Breeze

A toucan tells a funny story,
Of hedgehogs who chase after glory.
The breeze giggles as it flows,
Carrying tales of whimsical woes.

A small bluebird trips on a leaf,
Causing all to burst with grief.
But laughter rings through skies so blue,
As the frog croaks, 'Join us too!'

Wombats wobble, doing the jig,
While one considers a dance so big.
Their antics charm the drifting air,
And tickle hearts without a care.

Underneath the starlit dome,
Each creature calls this place their home.
The winds hold secrets, warm and bright,
In this realm of laughter's light.

Chronicles of the High-Hugging Giants

Gigantic trees share hearty roars,
With branches stretching, they open doors.
Each giant hugs a neighbor tight,
Creating shadows in the night.

Their whispers fill the chirping sky,
As long limbs wave, like hands up high.
A tall tale spills from barky lips,
Of squirrels on adventurous trips.

They challenge squirrels to a race,
With wobbly roots, and leafy grace.
But oh! One slips and tumbles down,
To land right in the giant's crown.

They roar with laughter, every beast,
Enjoying snacks, a leafy feast.
In a world where giggles reign,
High-huggers dance, avoiding pain.

Gatherings of the Winged Wonders

The birds unite in joyous song,
Their vibrant squawks, where they belong.
A parakeet tells of a prank,
While a crow laughs and starts to flank.

They gather 'round the tall oak tree,
Where pigeons nod in harmony.
One flaps wings too wide, oh dear!
And lands right on a startled deer!

In circles, they spin and glide,
Each flapping wing a playful ride.
With chirps and giggles, they create,
A symphony that feels just great.

As dusk rolls in, they share a feast,
With seeds and bugs, a tasty beast.
The evening ends in feathered cheer,
In the canopy, they hold it dear.

Serenade of the Swaying Stems

In a forest where the branches sway,
The critters dance and leap all day.
A squirrel did a jig upon a vine,
While owl hooted, 'Is that a sign?'

A rabbit tried to balance high,
With acorns flying like popcorn in the sky.
The raccoon rolled like a fluffy ball,
And shouted, 'I will not fall!'

The vines began to twist and twirl,
As hedgehogs donned their finest pearl.
With each swish and playful shove,
They formed a gang, calling it 'The Love.'

Laughter echoed through the trees,
As all joined in with goofy ease.
From leaf to leaf, they flew in cheer,
A symphony that all could hear!

Freedom in the Forgotten Forks.

Up high where the branches meet,
The birds all gathered for a treat.
A crow shared tales of nuts and crackers,
While the blue jays hooted like silly quackers.

In the forks, a chipmunk with flair,
Sipped from cups of dew without a care.
He spilled a bit, oh what a sight!
Caught in a splash, he took flight!

A frog hopped by in a tiny boat,
Made from leaves, floating like a goat.
He wobbled and bobbed, oh what a dive,
"Can I join?" asked a bee, buzzing alive!

In that place where shadows play,
The friends would frolic and sway all day.
Against the wind, they danced and spun,
For in their hearts, they had pure fun!

Whispers Among the Leaves

Under the rustle of leafy sound,
The giggles of critters could be found.
A lizard wore a tie so bright,
Claiming it was his fashion right!

Amid the branches, a squirrel declared,
"Let's have a contest, who's not scared?"
But as they climbed, the breeze did tease,
And off they tumbled with silly ease.

A wise old tree laughed with each fall,
"Just look at us, we're having a ball!"
Fairies sprinkled glitter in delight,
As they sprawled 'neath the stars at night.

So join the fun, dear friends and foes,
With every rustle, as laughter grows.
In whispers shared, a giggle leaves,
Among the branches, beneath the eaves!

Skyward Journeys

With a swing and a swoosh, they took to the air,
Where the breeze tickled tails and ruffled their hair.
The raccoon donned goggles, ready to glide,
While a busy bee buzzed, 'This is my ride!'

Through fluffy clouds and the sun's warm gleam,
They flew on adventure, chasing a dream.
An owl kept watch with a wink and a nod,
While munching on snacks that he deemed quite odd.

The heights brought giggles; oh what a race!
A leap and a twirl in the open space.
As they soared high, with hearts full of cheer,
Each giggle echoed, bringing friends near.

In the end, as stars softly blink,
They settled down and began to think.
With joy and laughter, they made their mark,
In the vast sky, slicker than a shark!

Under the Sunlit Trellis

Nestled in leaves where giggles grow,
A squirrel in socks steals the show.
Chasing his tail, oh what a sight,
Tangled in branches, he takes flight.

Birds wear hats, quite the affair,
Singing off-key, without a care.
A bunny joins in, slips on a vine,
Dancing around like he drinks fine wine.

The sun peeks through, a wink and a grin,
As laughter erupts from the forest's chin.
With peanut-shaped clouds, they take a break,
Playing charades with each silly quake.

Chronicles of the Crowned Giants

Underneath giants with crowns made of dew,
A march of ants wearing tiny shoes.
They gather round for a royal decree,
To dance through the glades, oh frolic with glee.

The branches shake as they stomp with delight,
A caterpillar twirls, what a charming sight!
With acorn cups raised high to the sun,
A ruckus erupts, oh, the playful fun!

As shadows stretch long, they chase the soft breeze,
Swinging from roots, hanging off trees.
With laughter that echoes, nature's sweet song,
The crowned giants chuckle, they all get along.

Laughter among the Limbs

In the cool shade where the critters play,
A raccoon juggles berries, hip-hip-hooray!
With a flip and a flop, he drops one loud,
And the brook giggles softly, oh how it's proud.

A deer in a tutu, doing a spin,
The frogs start to croak, oh let the fun begin!
Each leaf bursts with chuckles, what a wild scene,
As the wind whispers secrets, crisp and keen.

Twisting and twirling, they jump to the beat,
The laughter grows louder, oh what a treat!
Each nook, every cranny, filled with delight,
In the heart of the woods, on this marvelous night!

The Dance of Swaying Sprouts

Tiny sprouts shimmy, shaking all round,
They wiggle and giggle, never will drown.
Each blade of grass joins in the spree,
Bouncing and flouncing, wild as can be.

The flowers wear shades, too cool to be shy,
As bees start to hum, it's a lively high.
Butterflies flutter, leading the way,
In this garden party, they dance and sway.

With roots all entwined, they party in style,
While worms in their bow ties slide slick and agile.
In harmony blooming, a merriment feast,
Where the dance of the sprouts never seems to cease.

Skylit Stories from the Timberline

In the branches high, cats play tag,
Squirrels dress up in a leafy rag.
A parrot's joke makes one owl snort,
While rabbits dance, a wild court.

A raccoon wearing a hat too big,
Fields of nuts make him dance a jig.
They gossip about a lost shoe,
While the crow cackles, 'Oh, what a view!'

The wind whispers secrets to the leaves,
A rabbit sneezes, while giggling weaves.
The sun beams down, a spotlight bright,
As critters join for a comedic fright.

Under the stars, the night unfolds,
A tale of acorns and bravery bold.
With laughter echoing through the night,
The treetop life is a fanciful sight.

Breezes of the Canopy Keepers

A chatterbox monkey swings with flair,
While a turtle reports from his comfy chair.
Funny tales spin in the evening glow,
As fireflies twinkle, putting on a show.

The skunk tells tales in the soft moonlight,
Of a hedgehog dressed up, what a sight!
Squirrels giggle, tossing pinecones high,
As the owl hoots, 'Yet another lie!'

Chirping crickets join the fun parade,
While a bushy-tailed fox serenely played.
A dance off sparks, the laughter implodes,
With a breeze of joy, nature explodes.

Beneath the stars, the laughter rings,
In a world where everyone swings.
Together they share a quirky fate,
In the canopy's warmth, they celebrate.

Legends of the Forest Heights

Upon the limb, a spider spun,
The funniest story of the forest fun.
A badger claims he can outsmart a bee,
While the bee buzzes back, 'You wish, not me!'

The raccoons plot a late-night raid,
With hilarious antics, a grand charade.
Knocked over cans, a clanging noise,
Leaves all the critters with giggling joys.

From acorns to nuts, they laugh and play,
As the sun sets low, turning gold to gray.
With whispers of secrets high in the trees,
Tickles of joy dance on the breeze.

The forest thrives on laughter's cheer,
Each creature knows the fun is near.
Legends blossom in the oak tree shade,
Where giggling memories are lovingly made.

Flights of Fancy in Green Realms

The butterflies chatter, dress in bright hues,
While the chipmunks debate over what to choose.
A frog stands tall, as wise as a sage,
With stories of laughter on every page.

A squirrel forgot where his acorn lies,
While an owl chuckles, barely hiding his cries.
The raccoons conspire, a plot so silly,
To paint the fence with a splash of willy-nilly.

High in the branches, the shadow of fun,
As dragonflies dance, under the sun.
Each fluttering leaf tells a story shared,
Of laughter and joy, and how much they dared.

In this green realm, dreams take flight,
Creatures unite in the cool moonlight.
With swirls of giggles and laughter's call,
Fancy adventures enchant one and all.

The Life Above the Ground

Up high on branches, we swing and play,
Squirrels throw acorns in a cheeky way.
With every leap, our laughter soars,
Dodging clouds and opening doors.

The birds they chatter, gossip all day,
While we munch on berries in a cabaret.
A dance in the leaves, oh what a sight,
We twirl and giggle in morning light.

The wind plays tunes as it zips on by,
Tickling our toes, and making us sigh.
We wear crowns made of twigs, feeling so grand,
Living our dreams in this leafy land.

So join the fun, don't be a bore,
In our leafy realm, there's always more.
With a hop and a skip, come up with us,
Life's a hoot when you fly without fuss.

Aerial Adventures Under Starlit Canopies

Under the stars, we glide and zoom,
A flash of fur brightens the gloom.
The moon is our guide, so big and round,
As we play hide and seek without a sound.

Branches like trampolines, we bounce so high,
With a whoop and a holler, almost touch the sky.
The owls they hoot and the crickets sing,
In this night of mischief, we're the wild kings.

Swinging with ease from leaf to leaf,
Don't look down, or you'll lose belief.
A slip and a tumble, we laugh with glee,
A night under stars for you and me!

So grab your gear for a nighttime spree,
Adventure awaits, just wait and see.
With giggles and wiggles, through the trees we race,
Aerial antics in our hidden place.

Gatherings of the Forest Folk

Under the canopy, the folk all meet,
For a dance with the beetles, oh what a treat.
With mushrooms as snacks and nectar to sip,
We twirl and we leap, lose ourselves in the trip.

The raccoons juggle while the bunnies cheer,
With a tap of a toe, everyone draws near.
In the heart of the woods, we wear our best hats,
A merry parade of all furry friends and chats.

The frogs play the rhythms, the crickets the tunes,
As we stomp and we clap 'neath the light of the moons.
Each creature a star in our whimsical show,
Spreading joy through the forest, let the laughter flow.

So come one, come all, to the grand forest ball,
Where the fun never ends, and there's room for all.
With a wink and a grin, we'll dance till we drop,
In this gathering of friends, the joy never stops.

Secrets in the Sylvan Sea

High above the ground, in our leafy boat,
We sail through the branches, what a fun note.
With whispers of mischief in the air we share,
Secrets of the forest, floating without a care.

The squirrels they gossip while the bugs debate,
Who's the stealthiest hero, who's the best mate?
We watch and we chuckle, hidden from view,
In this vibrant theater, there's always something new.

Dreams drift like leaves on a dappled stream,
As we conjure our plans, oh, how they gleam.
In this sylvan escape, we map out the prize,
Unfolding great jokes, much to our surprise.

So grab onto a branch, let the laughter seize,
Secrets of the treetops swirl like a breeze.
With every guffaw, we rise and we soar,
In this whimsical world, who could ask for more?

The Upper Canopy Chronicles

Squirrels in suits with briefcase flair,
Juggling acorns in the crisp, cool air.
Birds on branches, having a feast,
Debating which worm is the prime cheese least.

Chattering monkeys play tag in the trees,
Dropping their snacks with such reckless ease.
They swing and they laugh, a wild parade,
While a sloth looks on, in the shade he's laid.

A raccoon wearing sunglasses, oh so chic,
His dance moves are silly, they're at their peak.
With each little twist and hilarious shout,
His forest friends cheer him, they can't live without.

In the canopy high, where the giggles sound,
Every critter's a jester, merrily crowned.
Life's one big circus up high in the trees,
Where laughter rings out on the light summer breeze.

Between the Branches and Dreams

Napping owls who hoot in a sleepy rhyme,
Dream of midnight snacks, it's snacky time!
While raccoons in pajamas raid the trees,
Collecting odd treasures with such deft ease.

Glowworms gather for a glow-in-the-dark show,
While frogs hop along, they steal the glow!
The fireflies join in with twinkling lights,
Creating a disco under the moonlit nights.

A parrot on roller skates, oh what a sight!
Spreading the news with a squawky delight.
While swinging monkeys grin as they swing,
Plotting their next funny, wild, zany fling.

Under the branches, pure chaos reigns,
With giggling critters that drive one insane.
Each day is a journey, so wacky and grand,
In the world where dreams and laughter go hand in hand.

Whims of the Wistful Wanderers

A hedgehog with goggles, oh what a scheme,
Slides down a sapling, a wacky dream!
While rabbits wear helmets, they giggle and race,
Through flowers and bushes, they laugh and embrace.

A llama on stilts states, "Look at me now!"
As he teeters and totters, making a vow.
With a wink at the trees, he stumbles with flair,
Bringing joy to the crowd with each perilous scare.

The butterflies dance in a playful parade,
While spiders in top hats offer sweet lemonade.
They sip and they chuckle in fancy attire,
As chubby-cheeked chipmunks join in with a choir.

In the whimsy of woods, the laughter runs wild,
Every creature a jester, each one a child.
In this crazy bough circus, the fun never ends,
Where each twist and turn feels like long-lost friends.

Meditations in the High Canopy

Wise trees whisper secrets, ancient and bold,
As squirrels debate stories, both new and old.
A fox with a vision board charts his great fate,
Believing he'll find the perfect acorn plate.

With pine cones as pillows, the critters unwind,
While a rabbit named Pip sorts the dreams of his kind.
"Next year," he declares, "I'll run for the moon!"
But he snoozes in sunbeams, dreaming of June.

Chattering birds practice their stand-up routine,
With punchlines that crack up their leafy green scene.
And the tree frogs do croak their most classic jokes,
Sending ripples of laughter through all the tree folks.

Each nutty explorer finds joy in this space,
Amidst the high branches, they celebrate grace.
In the meditative chaos of canopy fun,
Life's beautiful mischief shines bright like the sun.

Fables of the Fragrant Foliage

A squirrel donned a tiny hat,
He danced upon a green branch flat.
With acorns flying everywhere,
He pointed to the sky, quite a flair.

The birds chimed in with squawky tunes,
As rabbits hopped beneath the moons.
They giggled as they played their games,
Creating legends with funny names.

A wise old owl gave them a glare,
"Keep it down, or I won't share!"
But all the critters just laughed out loud,
Their joy was echoing, soft yet proud.

So if you wander where the green trees sway,
You might just catch their playful play.
For in the branches, stories brew,
Of funny friends and their silly crew.

Nature's Refuge in the Emerald Heights

Up in the trees, a raccoon rode,
On the back of a turtle, quite a load.
They zipped through the leaves, what a sight!
While squirrels cheered in sheer delight.

A parrot joined, squawking a jest,
"This ride's the best, who needs to rest?"
The turtle chuckled, slow but wise,
"Adventure is sweeter, just look at the skies!"

A feast was planned on a giant leaf,
With berries and nuts, beyond belief.
The gang set up their picnic spot,
Laughing so hard, they forgot the plot.

They toasted to friendship, funny and true,
As ants joined in for a bite or two.
Up in the heights where laughter reigns,
Nature's refuge never wanes.

Beneath the Canopy of Dreams

Under the leaves, a big bear snoozed,
While small critters danced, they were amused.
A raccoon tapped his tiny shoe,
Singing a tune that was quite askew.

A hedgehog rolled in a ball of glee,
"Roll with me, it's fun, you'll see!"
The song grew louder, a merry cheer,
While the dozing bear just curled and sneered.

Suddenly spiraled, a brilliant breeze,
Tickling the toes of all with ease.
They chortled and chuckled, a hilarious sight,
While overhead, the sun grew bright.

So if you see shadows dance and sway,
Know that beneath, they're having their play.
In dreams of laughter, in joy they roam,
Within the canopy, there's always home.

Secrets of the Skyward Realm

A dragonfly wore a monocle neat,
Claiming to know every garden sweet.
He buzzed around with fanciful flair,
While frogs croaked out tunes without care.

The frogs and bees held a contest too,
To see who could jump the highest view.
The dragonfly judged with a chuckle loud,
"Just try not to scare the clouds!"

A spider spun webs, a glorious stage,
Sipping dew drops, he'd turn the page.
With each little move, a comedy grew,
As a beetle tripped, and squeaked, "Oh boo!"

So when you think of the heights so grand,
Remember the laughter that's close at hand.
In the skyward realm where secrets dwell,
Funny friends have stories to tell.

Soaring Spirits in the Green

Up in the branches, the squirrels do prance,
They wear little hats, a comical dance.
With acorns in pockets and jokes in the air,
They giggle and chatter without a care.

Birds chirp in chorus, a wild, feathery band,
While raccoons in tuxedos join in on the stand.
The leaves rustle softly, as if they all cheer,
For the antics of critters, oh, what a sphere!

A maple tree shakes, with a laugh so deep,
As strap-happy rabbits form a line in a leap.
Together they swing from the branches so free,
In this leafy dominion, pure joy is the glee.

At sunset they gather, a wild celebration,
With fruit cake and cookies, a big jubilation.
In this green-hued kingdom where mischief runs wild,
The spirits of fun are forever beguiled.

Guardians of the Upper Realm

High in the canopy, with capes made of leaves,
The owls watch over, dispensing their cleaves.
With wise little winks and a hoot that's a laugh,
They guard all the goodies — it's quite the best half.

The raccoons patrol with their bandit-like flair,
Stealing the berries that float through the air.
They giggle and snicker, their masks firmly glued,
In a mission so bold, but always in good mood.

The nimble young chipmunks provide their own flair,
With tiny capes flapping, they dash everywhere.
Defenders of laughter, in shadows they spy,
On the jokes of the forest, they won't ever die.

A grand jamboree, each evening well planned,
With firefly lanterns sparking the land.
In this humorous kingdom, the daft are the wise,
For laughter's the treasure that never defies.

Harmony Among the Branches

In the tangle of limbs where the sunlight beams,
Creatures concoct their most whimsical dreams.
The parrot is painting a mural so bright,
While the rabbits are juggling with sheer delight.

The fox brings the snacks, a picnic galore,
With cheese made of twigs, who could ask for more?
The ants put on plays with leaves for the stage,
In this chaotic haven, there's no such thing as age.

Beneath swinging vines, they dance in a line,
The frogs in tuxedos croak songs so divine.
With laughter and joy, the hours drift away,
In this merry sanctuary, they frolic and play.

As Zephyr whirls by with a chuckle and spin,
The branches all sway, a joy to be in.
Though life may be silly, it's never a bore,
In this tree-top harmony, there's always much more.

Mythos of the Tree-dwellers

Once was a time when a wise old tree,
Told tales of hedgehogs with fears of a bee.
With shrieks and some giggles, they ran all around,
A sight to behold, in laughter they drowned.

The wise tree's roots, like anchors in soil,
Listened to squirrels plot mischief and toil.
Why steal just one acorn, they wondered aloud,
When the big raccoon is lugging up a crowd?

The notion that legends were born in the boughs,
Became common knowledge among the wise cows.
They chuckled and mooed at the follies they found,
Beneath their green canopy, hilarity crowned.

Even the wind joined the flights of their fables,
As it wove through the branches and danced on the tables.
In this world of wonders where laughter's held dear,
The myth of the tree-dwellers brings joy, it's quite clear!

The Ascending Path of Nature's Nomads

Up in the boughs, the squirrels play,
Chasing their tails, in a nutty ballet.
With acorns and laughter, they frolic around,
Making a ruckus, oh what a sound!

The raccoons join, with masks on their eyes,
Planning a heist, oh what a surprise!
They scale the trunks, with stealthy grace,
While the wise old owl just rolls his face.

A parrot squawks jokes, in a raucous sound,
Telling puns that leave all earthbound.
A monkey swings by and says with a grin,
"Your humor's so dry, I see it's a sin!"

But as night falls, they gather in peace,
Sharing their stories, no need for a lease.
Under the stars, the laughter will cease,
In the trees, nature's jesters find their ease.

Sagas of the Sylvan Sojourners

A chipmunk in boots wants to roam the woods,
Declares himself king of the neighborhood goods.
With a tiny crown made of twigs and of leaves,
He raises his voice and commands—"Who believes?"

The rabbits are laughing, they start up a dance,
Silly hop along, giving his reign a chance.
"Royal decree! Everyone twirl!"
As a hedgehog stumbles, and they all start to whirl.

An old tortoise, slow but wise,
Blessed them with tales of ancient skies.
"Do take care, kids, of nuts in the rain,
They become slippery and cause quite the pain!"

But frolicsome friends in their joyous spree,
Know laughter is king, as happy hearts decree.
In the laughter of nature, life's burdens take flight,
Forever they wander, from morning to night.

Murmurs of the Majestic Trees

The trees whisper secrets to those who will hear,
Of branches that waved like an old pioneer.
They chuckle at storms, how they dance in the breeze,
And gossip of critters climbing with ease.

A beaver with plans, a dam in his sights,
Thinks he's an architect with grand design flights.
But his assistant, a duck, quacks loud for a break,
"Need a snack now! Enough of this make!"

While shadows of owls blink in and out,
The wisdom of ages replaces their doubt.
"Never fear the fall! Just spread wide your wings!
Life's much too short, embrace all the flings!"

And the trees roar with laughter, the tales they could tell,
Of creatures in mishaps and all will do well.
In the hush of the woods, their stories are spun,
In the laughter of leaves, and the warmth of the sun.

Beyond the Branches, Into the Clouds

A crow in a top hat thinks he's a chap,
Struts through the forest; he's taking a nap.
With dreams of a party on a roof made of blooms,
He thinks he can rival the life of cartoons!

A striped cat approaches, all swagger and flair,
"Coming to party? It's quite the affair!"
He juggles with pinecones and spins in delight,
While a porcupine giggles, trying to take flight.

With acorns as snacks, they toast to their highs,
The laughter erupts as the sun starts to rise.
Together they dance, forgetting the ground,
With merriment swirling, oh what joy they found!

Eventually, they sway and tumble in fun,
As clouds gather round, in a dazzling run.
Let the world below, with its worries and frowns,
Know joy's found aloft, where hilarity crowns!

Woodland Whispers and Windy Lessons

In the woods of twigs and leaves,
A squirrel played a game of thieves.
He hid acorns in a nutty spree,
But forgot where he buried three!

The owls hooted with glee and cheer,
While rabbits laughed from ear to ear.
"You'd think a squirrel's smart as gold,
But watch him as he fumbles bold!"

A feathered friend took a wild dive,
Chasing a worm, felt so alive.
But slipped and landed in some moss,
And now he's known as funny boss!

So, if you trot through leafy ways,
Remember to chuckle through your days.
For woodland wisdom is quite a jest,
And laughter is what nature loves best!

Adventures in the Arbor Archipelago

Swinging high on branches wide,
A monkey slipped—oh what a ride!
He tumbled down with style and flair,
Foxes laughed, "Did you plan that air?"

Parrots squawked, 'Look at him fall!',
He bounced back up, gave a call.
"One more try, I'll reach that vine!"
But tripped on roots, oh so divine!

A turtle exclaimed with a wink,
"Quick critters move, but slow ones think!"
The monkey chuckled, shared the fun,
In this chaos, no race to run!

Across the leaves, in the sun's dance,
Every creature took a chance.
Laughter echoed through the air,
In the archipelago, we had no care!

Secrets of the Sun-Drenched Canopy

In the canopy where sunlight beams,
A lizard plotted silly schemes.
He wore a hat made of a leaf,
Pretending to be the forest chief!

The butterflies giggled as he pranced,
Doing a jig, they joined the dance.
"Dance all day and laugh we must,
In the sun, it's only fair we trust!"

A cricket jumped keen with great zest,
"Who said the forest can't be a fest?"
They celebrated squeaks and wiggles,
With funny moves and laughter giggles!

As shadows danced on the ground low,
Every furry friend put on a show.
The secrets held in sunlit charm,
Was fun, friendship, and no alarm!

Flights of Fancy Among the Fronds

Up in the fronds, where fancies fly,
A bird tried to sing, oh so shy.
But tripped on a branch, fell with a squawk,
A raccoon chortled, shared a talk!

"Don't worry, my dear, those in the skies,
Sometimes trip too, just look and rise!"
They laughed and shared seeds from a stash,
A feathery friend sprouted with flash!

The wind chimed in, with a gentle tease,
"Float like a leaf, sway with the breeze!"
From branch to branch, with ribbit and coo,
Their funny flights became the view!

So gather, dear friends, for giggles abound,
In the flights of fancy, joys are found.
Among the fronds, let laughter sing,
For every misstep, joy will bring!

Feathered Friends and Branching Paths

In a treehouse high where giggles flow,
Squirrels play hide and seek with a crow.
A parrot wears glasses, quite the sight,
While the owl keeps score, into the night.

The raccoon tells jokes, they're witty and grand,
As the chipmunks clap and form a band.
But watch for the branch that leans the wrong way,
It's a bumpy ride down—oh, what a display!

The woodpecker drums, a wild serenade,
While rabbits hop in time, unafraid.
A friendship formed in the warm sunlight,
Under leafy canopies, all feels just right.

With laughter and chatter, they savor each day,
Adventurers peering in such a silly way.
The forest is vibrant, a canvas of cheer,
With feathered friends cheering, let's all persevere!

High Above the Earth

Swinging from branches, the monkeys tease,
While giggles ripple like a summer breeze.
A kite-flinging frog leaps up with a cheer,
While the sun winks down, 'This place is dear!'

An eagle soars past with a silly grin,
While the hedgehog shouts, 'Let the fun begin!'
The trees sway and dance, a party indeed,
With critters all clad in colors so freed.

Flying from treetop to the ground down below,
The squirrels race fast but the tortoise is slow.
Yet everyone knows, it's the heart that will win,
In the carnival canopy, let the fun begin!

Jumping and playing, they live for the thrill,
In their paradise high, it's a magical chill.
And with each new adventure, they find humor's art,
In each little moment, they take to heart.

Falling Stars

When night settles in, the fireflies glow,
Hopping from leaf to leaf, moving slow.
A comet streaks past with a goofy laugh,
While the raccoon yells, 'Let's all make a gaffe!'

The owls start to hoot, a whimsical tune,
While crickets chirp softly beneath the moon.
But watch out below for the odd acorn drop,
As you chuckle and dance, you can't stop the bop!

Shooting stars tumble like marbles from the sky,
In a twirl of surprise, the rabbit asks why.
The friends gather round with wide-open eyes,
A night filled with magic, laughter, and sighs.

Once the show ends, they all settle down,
With dreams of tomorrow in the forest town.
Life in the trees, with each giggle and cheer,
Becomes brighter and warmer with friends gathered near.

Echoes of the Woodland Wanderers

In a glen where the wildflowers bloom and play,
A raccoon spins stories of his fun day.
The bunnies erupt with laughs and delight,
As the chipmunks join in, their eyes shining bright.

The tree trunks hum tunes, old tales they weave,
While leaves rustle gently, the forest believes.
An echo of laughter, a melody sweet,
Dances through branches, a rhythm with feet.

With every new story, a giggle starts rolling,
Of tales 'bout a bear who can't stop bowling.
The mood's light and merry, under skies so fair,
As each forest creature adds to the flair.

And so they gather, with joy in their eyes,
In a woodland theatre, beneath painted skies.
With echoes of laughter, the night comes to stay,
In a realm made for fun, let's watch how we play!

The Journey of Leaf and Wing

Two leaves took a ride on the back of a breeze,
They giggled and swirled, doing as they please.
A butterfly swooped in, all colors so grand,
Together they traveled, a whimsical band.

Past rivers and rocks, through the sunlit trees,
They found the best routes, avoiding the bees.
Singing out loud, in the afternoon sun,
They laughed at the squirrels who just couldn't run.

They tumbled and twisted; a game of hide and seek,
In a world full of magic, not just for the meek.
A dragonfly spun tales that made the heart race,
With gleeful adventures, a joyful embrace.

As the day starts to fade, they float down with grace,
Finding peace in the leaves, it's their favorite place.
In the quiet, they chuckle, sharing what they've seen,
Life in the trees, so funny and keen.

Hideouts of the Feathered Seekers

In the crook of a branch, a bird takes a nap,
With feathers of blue, he's lost in a clap.
A squirrel runs by, in his acorn-filled hat,
Daring to dance while the bird snores, 'What's that?'

A ruckus ensues as the worms start to giggle,
They twist and they turn, a wormy little wiggle.
"Oh, look at that fluff, so plump and so wise!"
"His feathers are stylish, but he dreams of pies!"

They plot through the branches, a feast to prepare,
"Let's lure him away! With a pie in the air!"
But the bird wakes up, fluffing out all his pride,
Catching the scent of the pie, oh, how he sighed!

They all share the treat, with crumbs left to spare,
Singing and laughing, without a single care.
And as day turns to dusk, the tales will unfold,
In hideouts of laughter, their secrets retold.

The Arachnid's Web of Stories

A spider spun silk, such a delicate case,
With stories of flies sewn in delicate lace.
"Come hear the buzz of my fabulous life,
How I dance on my web, avoiding all strife!"

A beetle approached, with a knack for a pun,
"Is your web made from sugar? I'm sweet on the run!"
They both chuckled hard at the humor of fate,
In the big tangled web where they both like to sate.

Then came a young moth with a twinkle in eye,
"Tell me your stories, oh wise one up high!"
With laughter, they wove all the tales of the night,
While fireflies flickered, adding spark to their light.

As dawn started breaking, a chorus rang clear,
The spider just smiled, with a wink full of cheer.
"We've spun tales together, from dusk until dawn,
Let's gather again!" And the friends carried on.

Explorers of the Green Kingdom

Two chums on a quest, with their hats slightly skewed,
They marched through the forest, where odd creatures brood.
"Did you see that tree?" one exclaimed with a grin,
"It's wearing a coat made of leaves and of skin!"

They stumbled on squirrels, who were planning a show,
A circus of acorns with a juggler below.
"Grab a seat on that stump, and let's enjoy the feat!"
They clapped and they cheered at the acorn parade.

The duo then rolled, down the hill full of grass,
Where turtles were racing, but nobody could pass.
"Hey, what if we cheer for the slowest of them?"
And with that, they whispered, "Go, Carl! You're our gem!"

At last, they found treasure, a berry so bright,
They feasted together and laughed till it's night.
With explorers' hearts, they ventured once more,
In the kingdom of green, always ready to roar!

Legends in the Light-dappled Woods

In the shade of tall trees, where sunlight leaks through,
Legends are whispered, both silly and true.
A raccoon named Rufus, with a knack for a snack,
Tells tales of the moon and the stars on his back.

He claimed he once danced with a skunk in a hat,
And they twirled through the trees, oh, imagine that!
While owls rolled their eyes, trying hard not to laugh,
They wise-cracked about if it had been a giraffe.

With creatures all gathered, the jokes flew around,
Who knew that a rabbit could make such a sound?
"I'm hopping to fame! Join my show in the glen!"
And with that, they howled, "Let the legends begin!"

As dusk painted skies with a mischievous grin,
They spun all their yarns, let the laughter begin.
In the light-dappled woods, where stories collide,
The friends share their legends, with joy as their guide.

The Climb to Celestial Breezes

Up we go, to the leafy crown,
Holding tight, don't look down!
A raccoon chuckles, what a sight,
As we swing with all our might!

Squirrels gossip, tails in twist,
"Don't lose your grip, or you might miss!"
A babbling brook below does cheer,
While birds sing loud for all to hear.

Branches sway, a dance so grand,
We sway back and forth, can't understand.
We laugh till tears fall like rain,
In this high world, we feel no pain!

At the top, what joy we find,
Clouds like candy, so sweet and kind.
With giggles echoing through the air,
Our treetop antics beyond compare!

Wonders of the Winding Vine

Through the vines, we slip and slide,
Giggling faster, can't run and hide!
A swing, a twirl, let's take the leap,
Who knew these vines would make us peep?

Bouncing like beans on a string,
Monkey laughter, oh what a fling!
With each twist, a new dare unfolds,
A story of pandemonium told.

We tumble and rumble, lost in cheer,
Spinning like tops, collecting cheer!
Oh, the mischief we leave behind,
In entangled fun, so well-defined!

At the end, we land with a crash,
Exhausted, giggling, what a bash!
The wonders of vines, our playground vast,
In this giggly jungle, our joy's amassed!

Dancers in the Sunlight

With sunbeams twinkling on our toes,
We frolic and spin, as the wind blows.
Caterpillars join our little show,
Twirl once more, oh what a glow!

The breeze plays tricks, rustles our hair,
We leap and dodge without a care.
A butterfly flutters by our side,
In this sunny dance, we can't hide!

The leaves above clap a catchy beat,
We prance and leap, can't feel defeat.
It's a festival in the green light,
With every giggle, we take flight!

As shadows grow long, our dance won't cease,
With friendship and laughter, we find sweet peace.
In the heartbeat of nature, we find our fun,
For we are the dancers, 'neath the bright sun!

Shadows of the Tallest Trees

Under the trees, we tiptoe slow,
Where giants loom, giving shadowy glow.
A wise owl hoots, "What's the fuss?"
While we stumble and giggle, full of trust!

A branch swings by with a playful sway,
"Watch out, or you might lose your way!"
We duck and laugh, what a surprise,
In search of mischief, we brave the skies!

A squirrel throws acorns, a cheeky prank,
We dodge and weave, our giggles dank.
With shadows stretching, the fun won't end,
In the tallest trees, we play and bend!

So let's embrace the humor here,
In leafy lanes, we dance and cheer.
Beneath these shadows, our joy took flight,
In the company of trees, it feels just right!

www.ingramcontent.com/pod-product-compliance
Lightning Source LLC
Chambersburg PA
CBHW071851160426
43209CB00003B/511